Animal Wor

MW01142907

Dolphins

Donna Bailey

RSVP
RAINTREE
STECK-VAUGHN
PUBLISHERS
The Steck-Vaughn Company

Austin, Texas

Dolphins live near the coast in
most of the oceans of the world.
Dolphins are mammals so they breathe air.
They give birth to young which drink
the mother dolphin's milk.

2

Dolphins have a smooth, sleek body that helps them glide easily through the water. They swim by moving their big tail flukes up and down.
They use their side flippers to steer and turn.

Most kinds of dolphins have jaws that
stick out and make a beak-like snout.
Above the upper jaw is the "melon" which
looks like a bulging forehead.
The melon is a mass of fatty tissue.

A dolphin breathes air through
a blowhole on top of its head.
When it dives, a dolphin closes
the blowhole and holds its breath.
It can dive as deep as 1,000 feet, but it needs
to surface every two minutes to breathe.

Dolphins love to roll and play in the waves.
They "porpoise" through the water, making
shallow dives and surfacing every
few minutes.

Dolphins play by swimming and diving
as a group.
Often a whole group will break the surface
of the water at the same time.
Dolphins can leap as high as 20 feet into
the air before diving back into the waves.

Dolphins are very intelligent creatures
and have large brains.
They talk to each other by making sounds.
When they are excited or afraid, they make
a high-pitched squeal or whistle.

Dolphins also make a clicking sound.
The sound is made inside the melon,
just below the blowhole.
Dolphins use these clicks as a kind of sonar.
The echo of the sounds bounces back from
schools of fish or other underwater objects.

Dolphins live together in a family group.
The group hunts for fish and squid to eat.
Some dolphin families join together
to make schools.

Dolphins look after sick or wounded
members of the school.
Sometimes a pair of dolphins may even
support a sick dolphin on their flippers.
They keep the sick dolphin near the surface
so that it can breathe above the waves.

Most dolphins mate during the spring.
Eleven or twelve months later,
the baby dolphin is born.
A baby dolphin is called a calf.

The calf is born underwater.
The mother pushes her calf to the surface
to take its first breath.
The newborn calf can swim and
breathe well only a few minutes
after birth.

Within the first day, the calf learns
to drink its mother's milk.
Another female dolphin often
helps the mother look after the calf.
The adult dolphins protect the calf from sharks.

A mother dolphin looks after her calf
for several years.
The calf follows its mother closely
for the first few weeks.
It often swims beside the fin on her back.
The water flows smoothly over the calf
as its mother swims.

Baby dolphins drink their mother's milk for
over a year after birth.
They start eating fish at about six months.
Even a full-grown dolphin may return to
its mother if it is afraid or unhappy.

16

Mother dolphins and their calves
usually swim together near the center
of a school of dolphins.
Small groups within a school usually swim,
dive, and feed together.
In some schools, there are hundreds of dolphins.

There are about 40 kinds of dolphins.
The common dolphin is found in oceans
all over the world, except in the polar regions.
This dolphin is about six feet long and
can swim as fast as 30 miles an hour.

The best-known dolphins are
the bottle-nosed dolphins.
They are often seen
doing tricks in water shows.
Their short beak makes them look
as if they are smiling.

Most bottle-nosed dolphins live
in coastal waters.
On this beach in Australia, the dolphins
sometimes come right up to the beach.
They are not afraid of people and often
make friends with tourists.

Dolphins are very intelligent and
can be trained easily.
Dolphins have been trained to find
torpedoes on the bottom of the sea,
to put mines on enemy ships, to detect
submarines, and to guard harbor entrances.

Dolphins in captivity are trained
to do tricks to entertain people.
Learning tricks probably keeps
the dolphins from getting bored
with living in a small pool.

22

These boutos are river dolphins.
Boutos live in the muddy waters
of the Amazon River.
They have a very long beak and can turn
their head around and sideways.

Most wild dolphins live in the sea.
This white-sided dolphin lives in
the Pacific Ocean.
The tall fin on its back is white and
its belly is white.

These right-whale dolphins also live
in the Pacific.
They don't have a fin on their back.
Right-whale dolphins hardly ever come
up to the beach.
They spend their time in the deep ocean.

Spinner dolphins have much longer beaks than bottle-nosed dolphins.
They live in schools in the eastern Pacific.
Many get tangled up in the drift nets of Japanese fishing fleets.

Spotted dolphins are also in danger from
drift nets in the eastern Pacific.
The netting is so thin that dolphins
can't detect it with their sonar.
Dolphins swim into the nets and
can't escape to get air, so they drown.

Pilot whales and killer whales are
the biggest dolphins.
Killer whales can grow as long as
30 feet and weigh several tons.

Dolphins are warm-blooded animals.
A fatty layer of blubber under their skin keeps
them warm in the cold water of the sea.
Some fishers hunt dolphins
for their meat and blubber.

Some fishers say that dolphins
eat the fish they want to catch.
The fishers use loud underwater noises
to frighten away the dolphins.

When dolphins are afraid, the whole school quickly swims away together.
The animals swim until they get tired and run out of breath.

When fishers drop nets to catch tuna,
they must be careful not to trap dolphins
swimming at the surface.
Some tuna fishers send out a diver
to help the dolphins escape through
special panels in the nets.